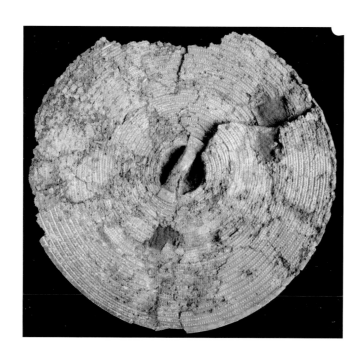

CEREMONY AND DISPLAY:
THE SOUTH CADBURY BRONZE AGE SHIELD

by John Coles, Stephen Minnitt and Andrew Wilson

Prospect of Camalet Castle. 15 Aug. 1723.   *Stukeley Del.*

1. *William Stukeley's drawing of Cadbury Castle in 1723*

Cadbury Castle is a 7.5 hectare multi-rampart Iron Age hillfort. Sited on a naturally steep-sided hilltop in south east Somerset it overlooks the present-day villages of South Cadbury and Sutton Montis. Standing some 80 metres above the surrounding countryside the hilltop has magnificent views to the north encompassing Glastonbury Tor and the Somerset Levels, the Mendip Hills, the Bristol Channel and, on a clear day, the coast of south Wales. The sequence of ramparts, constructed in the final centuries BC, remain impressive even today.

The site has long attracted interest (**1**). The earliest account of Cadbury Castle is by John Leland, an early 16th century antiquary, who wrote: *'sumtyme a famose toun or castelle, apon a very torre or hille, wunderfully enstrengtheid of nature, to the which be 2 enteringes up by very stepe way: one by north est, and another by south west......... In the upper parte of the coppe of the hille be 4 diches or trenches, and a balky waulle of yerth betwixt every one of them.'* Leland went on to say: *'The people can telle nothing ther but that they have hard say that Arture much resortid to Camalat.'* To this day Cadbury Castle is associated in the minds of many people with Arthur and Camelot.

Much of the visible archaeology dates to the last few centuries BC, the period when the ramparts were constructed (**2**). Cadbury Castle was the subject of a major programme of archaeological excavations directed by Leslie Alcock between 1966 and 1973, which revealed that the site had been occupied, on and off, over a period of four thousand years. A sequence of occupation from the Neolithic to the Anglo-Saxon period was uncovered. The earliest occupants were a small community of farmers, probably tilling the hilltop. From about 2500BC until 1150BC the evidence is limited to a number of distinctive bronze objects which reveal little about the nature of those living on the site. During the Late Bronze Age, the period from about 1150BC until 750BC, the evidence for occupation includes a small cluster of buildings, and the settlers left behind some potsherds and pieces of bronzework, as well as part of a gold bracelet. The construction of a major fortification in the Iron Age, in the centuries from about 400BC, involved a high level of organisation and resources. Within the defences there lived a thriving community.

The prehistoric period ended in a massacre, and parts of bodies were found strewn through the south west gateway. There followed a period when a Roman temple may well have been the primary feature of the hill and two occasions, the late 5th century and early 11th century AD, when the old Iron Age defences were refurbished and provided temporary refuge at times of uncertainty and threat.

The occupants of the hilltop throughout this remarkable sequence did not live in isolation. The land around was of importance to them for farming, hunting, timber and doubtless other resources. The South Cadbury Environs Project was established in 1995 to investigate evidence for the archaeology of the later prehistoric to Early Medieval periods in the landscape surrounding Cadbury Castle. The Project employed a variety of techniques including fieldwalking, geophysical survey, study of air photographs and selective excavation. One site chosen for excavation was a narrow spur, known as Milsom's Corner, below the south west entrance to the hillfort. The site proved to have a long and complex history from the Neolithic to the end of the Iron Age. Features

revealed included two sides of a Bronze Age rectangular enclosure formed by a ditch. The ditch, 1.5 metres deep, had cut through two earlier Bronze Age burials. Finds from the ditch were few, but intentionally placed bones, particularly cattle mandibles, were common suggesting that the site had served some kind of ritual function.

A sheet bronze shield was discovered in June 1997 in the upper fill of the angle formed by the two sides of the ditch. The discovery was wholly unexpected. Exposure of a small length of the rim of the shield revealed it to be in an extremely fragile state, so much so that it could not be excavated on site. The Somerset County Council Museums Service was contacted and arranged for conservators from Wiltshire County Council Conservation Service, Salisbury, to assist in the recovery of the shield.

2. *Aerial photograph of Cadbury castle from the south. The shield was found just to the west of the fort(bottom left of the photograph)*

Recovery and conservation

Bronze Age shields are extremely rare and the conservation of the South Cadbury shield demanded specialist treatment. When the conservators arrived on site, the soil had been cut back from around the shield leaving it sandwiched inside a pedestal of earth. The job of the conservators was to ensure that the fragile shield, within its soil block, was lifted and transported back to their laboratory in Salisbury where the painstaking process of micro-excavation and treatment could begin under controlled conditions. The soil block was tightly wrapped using bandages and then undercut using slate rippers to free it from the ditch deposits (**3**). Galvanised steel plates were inserted underneath which allowed the block to be slid onto a wooden board upon which it was carried from the site.

Back at the Conservation Centre in Salisbury conservator Andy Wilson began work. His first task was to ensure that the soil block was fully supported. Sand was poured into cracks within the soil and then a box was constructed around the block using the wooden board on which it had been lifted as its base. The block was tightly sealed with clingfilm and polyurethane foam was poured around it. Polyurethane foam expands to form a lightweight but rigid support, ideal in this instance since adding weight to the sizeable block of soil, already weighing more than 75kg, would have been a problem.

With the block now more stable it was time to see what lay inside. The block was taken to Salisbury District Hospital where staff in the Spinal Injuries Unit produced the first images of a near complete and highly decorated shield using x-radiography. The results were remarkable considering the shield was less than one millimetre in thickness and still buried in the block of soil. The x-radiographs provided technical information on the construction of the shield and its fittings and on its condition, both crucial to the conservation process (**4**).

3. *Conservators preparing to lift the shield from the site*

The x-radiographs highlighted cracks within the shield and variation in the corrosion, but excavation could begin with confidence working initially on the best preserved areas. Small wooden and metal handtools were used to peel away soil in layers down to the shield's surface.

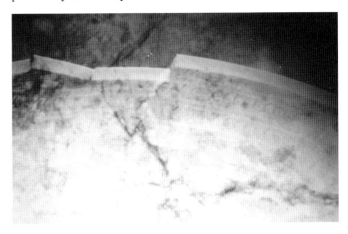

4. *X-ray of part of the rim of the shield*

Cotton swabs soaked in solvent were used to clean the surface detail. Each side was excavated in quadrants. Exposure of the shield in the first quadrant showed it to be lying front-face down and that it had suffered some distortion.

5. *Half of the back of the shield exposed during conservation*

Throughout treatment the soil block was kept moist to prevent it from drying out, shrinking and cracking which would have caused damage to the fragile shield (**5**). Normally excessive moisture is considered to be a threat to metalwork causing corrosion. However the first few fragments found showed that there was no possibility of the shield corroding further since no metal remained, with the exception of the ends of the handgrip. Lying in the soil at South Cadbury the bronze had been converted to brilliant blue-green corrosion products. In places these corrosion products were compact and preserved surface detail well, in other areas the surface was seriously disrupted. Cracks, some major and some hairline, ran across much of the shield and added significantly to its fragility.

Continuous records of context, technology and condition were made as work progressed. Plan drawings, recorded on a grid system, were traced at 1:1 onto plastic sheeting on a perspex board laid directly over the soil block. Photography and filming were used to document the process of conservation.

In order to clean and record its front the shield had to be turned over, not easy when dealing with something resembling a collapsed jigsaw puzzle. The exposed back of the shield was first 'faced' with overlapping strips of open-weave textile. This temporary facing layer was applied to the shield fragments with reversible adhesive to keep them in position and prevent slippage. A 'barrier layer' of aluminium foil was placed over the facing and polyurethane foam was poured in as moulded support up to the rim of the box. Once the polyurethane had solidified the box was turned over. The base board, which had now become the lid, was removed and the process of excavation repeated (**6**).

6. *Cleaning of the front of the shield by conservator Andy Wilson*

It became apparent very early on during treatment that the shield could only be displayed flat because of its fragmented condition. Only one face could be displayed. The other side would require total support and would become lost to view. A detailed record was therefore made which included photogrammetry, sponsored by GKN Westlands, enabling a computerised reconstruction to be made of the shield.

After considerable discussion the back of the shield was chosen as the side to be displayed since it showed the greatest amount of technical information. Also as the back was the side visible at the time of deposition this would help retain the original context of the shield. This decision, of course, required the shield to be turned over one final time. Prior to this, dyed textile was adhered as a facing layer to the front of the shield to hold the fragments together. A moulded support was constructed out of glass fibre polyester resin on which the shield would rest.

With the shield turned over and resting on its moulded support the temporary textile facing applied to the back of the shield was removed. The surface was finally cleaned using swabs soaked in solvent in preparation for the shield going on public display (**7**). Work on the shield was spread over the whole of the year 1998, and conservator Andy Wilson spent a total of 353 hours excavating, cleaning, stabilising and recording it.

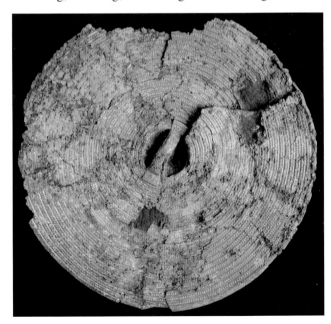

7. *The fully conserved back of the shield*

Description & technology of the shield

The South Cadbury shield is of a type well-known in Britain; about 20 or so exist at present, with a few others recorded but now lost to view. They occur from the north of Scotland to the river Thames in southern England, and the South Cadbury shield is the first known from the south-west of England (**8**). A peat bog at Yetholm in southern Scotland yielded three of these shields, all now in the National Museum of Scotland, and Yetholm is the name given to the type.

Yetholm-type shields are of sheet bronze, circular in shape and defined by a varying number of concentric ribs and rows of small bosses, with a central boss that hides a sturdy handle on the back of the shield (**9**). At the edge of the shield, the sheet metal is turned over to the front and hammered down to create a strong rim. The metal used for the shields was a high-tin bronze, that is, about 11-14% tin and the rest copper, with slight traces of other elements. The diameter of the South Cadbury shield is 665mm (26 inches), and there are 25 ribs and 25 rows of bosses; a few Yetholm-type shields are slightly larger and have a few more rib and boss rows, but most are smaller and with fewer rows.

The number of bosses on the South Cadbury shield was 6030, and only a few other shields had as many; one monster shield from Ayrshire has about 9200 small bosses in its 29 rows.

9. *One of the Yetholm shields from Scotland*

The small bosses on the South Cadbury shield are only 4mm diameter and they stand 1.6mm high; the ribs are 1.9mm high (**10**). The precision in production of these elements is very high. The central boss, about 110mm wide and 37mm high, was equally skilfully created (**11**). The sheet metal is only 0.6mm thick, and to make the

○ Yetholm-type Shield

8. *The distribution of Bronze Age shields in Britain and Ireland*

or were masterminded by one craftsman who imparted his skills to a very few workers. The production of the shield began with the preparation of a thin sheet of bronze, planished by hammer and flatter, then the central boss was created by punch and hammer, to be followed by the shaping of the ribs, from central boss outwards, then the rows of small bosses, and finally the turning of the rim, and attachment of handle and tabs through drilled holes (14). The tools used would include some form of compass, drill, hammer, punch and flatter. At all times, extreme care would be needed to ensure that the sheet was not perforated by over-heavy use of punch and hammer, and that the expression of grading outwards of ribs and boss rows was uniform.

10. *Close-up photograph of the rim, ribs and boss rows of the South Cadbury shield*

central boss the metal had to be hammered out to a thickness of only 0.4mm. The handle of the shield was made from a thicker piece of bronze sheet, folded over a core of tin to make a sturdy and heavy grip (12); this was rivetted onto the back of the shield behind the central boss so that the rivets merged with the innermost row of small bosses. Also rivetted onto the back of the shield were two metal tabs which would carry a leather strap (13).

All of these features of the South Cadbury shield are matched on the other Yetholm-type shields, although sizes and shapes may differ to a small degree. What is abundantly clear is the very high technical ability shown in the production of the shields, and it is quite likely that most of the shields came from one workshop

11. *The central boss of the shield*

12. *The handle of the South Cadbury shield*

In the actual work on the shields of Yetholm-type, we can see various places where the craftsman has made small adjustments in the position of bosses to compensate for errors in spacing; as a boss row neared completion, the worker would have to judge if, for example, he could fit eight, or nine, bosses into the remaining space. Sometimes he had to over-space or under-space the bosses to ensure a reasonably even and inconspicuous joining of the last boss beside the first boss of the row. Some speculation on the sequence of work listed above still exists, and we do not know the exact type of tools used in the work; we do not have Bronze Age compasses, and only a small number of punches, and we do not yet have any of the specialised flanged punches that we now think were needed to make the bosses uniform in width and depth.

Nor do we have much information about how the sheet bronze was supported during the work. One possibility is that the sheet was fastened to a bed of pitch, or laid on a bed of lead, either of which would give firm support yet yield to the pressure of the punch in accepting the sheet

bronze as it was carefully shaped downwards, rib by rib, boss by boss. Lead would have been very useful in the work but it is not clear if lead was available at the time when Yetholm-type shields were being made. Pitch, from various trees (pine) or tar, from others (birch), might have served the purpose.

13. *One of the tabs rivetted on the back of the South Cadbury shield*

Despite their thinness Yetholm-type shields are quite strong, as the ribs and rim give the bronze a rigidity against bending. The amount of metal needed for a shield was about 1000-1400g, so the handle had to be heavy to aid the person holding and using the shield. The handles tend to be rather narrow for our modern hands and they were probably equally narrow for Bronze Age people. This suggests that the shield, if used in battle against sword-bearing warriors, would have been difficult to manipulate, being held only by fingers pinched together on the handle. However, as objects of great beauty and brilliance the shields would be without equal. Taken together with the very high cost of material and the extreme technical skill, and time, needed for the production of shields, this suggests that these shields

were probably used for display and ceremony, and not for actual physical combat. To test this theory, experiments were carried out with copies of these shields, using copper sheet hardened to equal that of the Bronze Age bronze shields; a single blow with a bronze sword cut the replica in two (**15**). Shields were not backed with wood or leather in order to give them a more practical function. This is deduced from the size and means of attachment of the tabs and handgrip and the total absence of such evidence on those shields found in wet contexts where organic remains would have survived had they been present. It is likely that the Bronze Age warrior would use shields of leather or wood to defend himself; Bronze Age shields made of these substances have been found in peat bogs in Ireland.

15. *Replica shields being tested against slashing swords (The shield on the left is of leather, the other was of sheet copper)*

14. *Close-up photograph of ribs and boss rows of a Yetholm shield*

The context of the South Cadbury shield

Bronze Age shields overwhelmingly derive from wet contexts, and the South Cadbury shield is the sole exception to this pattern. Placed in rivers, lakes and bogs, shields have been discovered during dredging and drainage operations and peat extraction. They formed part of the widespread practice in the later Bronze Age of the ritual consignment of valuable metal objects to wet places which elsewhere in north west Europe included lurs (horns), helmets, swords and elaborate axes. The motivation behind this practice which permanently removed prestigious objects from society is unknown but was clearly very powerful. Could it have been to placate the gods or to ensure victory in battle or, perhaps, to express thanks for a victory just achieved?

Their places of deposition and the circumstances under which they have been found mean that we have little information on the events or rituals associated with the votive offering of shields. Accounts of early discoveries may contain some clues; for example, shields from Inghoe, Northumberland, and Harlech, Gwynedd, had been placed vertically on their edges, and five or six shields from Beith, Ayrshire, had been placed in a circle. A hoard of 16 shields found at Fröslunda, in southern Sweden, in 1985 had been laid into shallow water in a small bay of a very large lake. They were clustered together, overlapping, and must have been carried to their final resting place by boat.

Some of the British shields suffered damage in antiquity; in one instance the tabs were removed by cutting out triangular sections of a shield; in other instances shields were pierced by spearheads or perhaps slashed by rapiers or swords. It cannot be established with certainty whether these acts of damage occurred at the time of deposition or on an earlier occasion, but some, perhaps most, probably represent the 'killing' of the shields before they were placed in open water or reedy pools for what was intended to be eternity. Data on the function of shields prior to their deposition is also lacking. Were they made purely as sacrificial objects or, more likely, did they serve initially as objects signifying the power and prestige of those who possessed them? The evidence of repairs to a very few shields supports the possibility of some form of usage prior to their going to a watery grave.

Having been discovered during an excavation the circumstances of deposition of the South Cadbury shield is better understood than that of the others but many key questions remain unanswered. Placed front-down in the largely silted up angle of a ditch the shield had been violently stabbed three times, perhaps with a wooden stake. This act of destruction made three holes through the shield forcing metal down into the earth below. For the first time we can be certain that damage to a shield occurred at the time of deposition. The shield had also suffered a heavy blow to the rim but the timing of this is less certain.

The placing of the South Cadbury shield appears to have been an isolated event on the site; at least no associated or contemporary activity was recognisable in the archaeological record. Soil samples associated with the shield underwent pollen analysis in the hope that this would shed light upon the immediate environment. Although pollen preservation was poor it did show lime and holly to have grown in the vicinity, together with cereals, daisies and dandelions.

Traditionally, Yetholm-type shields are dated to the late Bronze Age, around 1000-800 BC. A programme of metal analyses on Yetholm-type shields was undertaken as part of the programme of research following the discovery of the South Cadbury shield. This work suggests that shields were made somewhat earlier than expected. It is likely that the South Cadbury shield was made, used and deposited sometime in the period 1200-1000BC, so the shield is 3200-3000 years old.

Interpretation of shields

Shields of Yetholm-type are entirely restricted to Britain and Ireland other than one Danish example. The continental European shields of the Bronze Age are decorated, and strengthened, by different arrangements of ribs and bosses, and sometimes by embossed bird-like designs. All of the shields are impressive in their technological sophistication and in their physical appearance - large, shiny and oozing prestige. That they were not everyday objects is clear from their fragility as well as from their places of deposition. The ceremonies in which they had a part are shrouded in mystery for us today, but a glimpse can be achieved by looking at a different kind of archaeological evidence, and from a different geographical region.

One of the features of the Bronze Age in southern Scandinavia is the presence on the hard rocks of the ancient coastlines of carvings, which depict a great variety of Bronze Age images. Carvings of boats are very abundant, as well as innumerable cupmarks which are small indentations made by pecking and grinding. Other carvings on the rocks are of animals, discs, humans, hands and feet, with smaller numbers of wheeled vehicles, nets or frames, ards, weapons and other items of personal equipment. These images often appear together, in a variety of combinations that seem to represent scenes of one sort or another. We do not know if these are, or were, real events or if they were mythological, perhaps asking Bronze Age gods for good weather, good crops, success in battle, victory over the odds in time of stress. Or perhaps they were thank offerings for past events, or maybe they commemorated certain persons or happenings.

16. *(upper) Rock carving from Ekenberg, Sweden (lower) Carving of a continental-type shield and sword on a slab from, Brozas, Cáceres, Spain*

Among the multitude of rock carvings are some, not many, that depict shields or shield-like images. Because the artist was confronted by rock rather than bronze, he or she could not hope to reproduce all of the ribs and bosses of metal shields, but could only show a representation of the shields by a few ribs and a few bosses. Nevertheless, the results are strikingly reminiscent of the Yetholm-type shields and not at all like the continental shield designs. This similarity suggests that some form of contact in ideas and perhaps in prestige objects took place between Britain and the northern lands of the continent. Furthermore, the carvings show some of the events in which shields had a role, whether symbolic or in reality. We will look at four examples of rock carvings.

Round shields with a central boss and concentric ribs, but no other bosses, are often depicted on the rocks of Sweden in particular; they might well represent another symbol, such as the sun, but at Ekenberg in eastern Sweden a disc is carved immediately beside a large sword which points directly at the disc (16). In view of the ritual 'killing' at South Cadbury and other sites, by sword or stake thrusts, this carving might show the relationship between defence and offense in Bronze Age imagery. The same relationship appears on a rock carving in Spain (16).

A number of rock carvings of human figures show the human body as a shield-like disc, with head and arms above and legs below (21). Some of the humans carry spears or axes, so perhaps these carvings, again, try to continue the idea of armed conflict, with weaponry and symbolic armour. It is quite possible that such body-protecting shields were meant to ward off evils

other than the simple ones of attack by actual combat.

Two Bronze Age rock carvings from western Sweden are much more explicit in the shield representations. A boat carving from Svenneby shows a large boat with elaborate prow and stern posts, a line of strokes, perhaps the crew, just over the gunwale, and two large humans standing amidships (17). Both have sword scabbards hanging from their waists, and one holds a battle-axe. The other holds a shield with bosses in a circle on the shield body. This carving may represent a war party moving purposely forward to battle, or may show some ceremonial arrival or departure with precious weaponry.

17. *Rock carving from Svenneby, Sweden*

A larger rock carving from Hede in the same area presents the shield image in greater abundance and in even more graphic detail (18). Above a large boat (partly destroyed) stands a male human, sword scabbard with hooked terminal hanging from his waist. With one hand

he holds a finely-detailed shield with ribs and bosses; this is a Yetholm-type. Near this warrior are other isolated shield designs as well as a human with horned helmet, an acrobatic figure falling backwards and a large human with arms raised in supplication. The whole panel demonstrates ceremony and display, the actions doubtless pre-determined and traditional and the objects of ostentatious wealth and prestige. What the whole process was meant to convey to the viewer, and the artist's role in it all, is not known to us today, but it must surely involve ritual behaviour and seek assurances or offer appreciations from powers that did not reside within the society but which were to be found in the other worlds both above and below the living - the sky and the water, the heavens and the underworld.

18. *Photograph and plan of a rock carving at Hede, Sweden (The central figure is 60 cm in height)*

New display, new product

The South Cadbury shield arrived at the Somerset County Museum, Taunton, in December 1998 and was placed on public display a short time afterwards (**19**). The process from discovery to display was one of co-operation between many parties, the landowners, the excavators, the conservators, various specialists, museum staff and the funding organisations. This, and in particular the outstanding work of the conservator, resulted in Andy Wilson and Wiltshire County Council Conservation Service winning the 1999 Museums and Galleries Commission Award for Conservation.

19. *The South Cadbury shield on display in the Somerset County Museum, Taunton*

20. *Label from Montgomery's Jersey Shield cheese*

The survival, conservation and research carried out on the shield was possible only because of the generosity of the landowner, Elizabeth Montgomery, and her family in donating the find to the Somerset County Museums Service very shortly after its discovery and while the object still lay unseen in the soil block. By doing so, grant sources for funding the work were opened up. It seems highly appropriate that when James Montgomery launched a new cheese made from the milk of the family's herd of Jersey cows, fed largely on grass from the slopes of Cadbury Castle, the shield should be used in both the name and marketing of that cheese. Montgomery's Jersey Shield went on sale in 2000 (**20**).

21. *Rock carving from Vitlycke, Sweden, of a human with shield-like body*

Further reading:

J M Coles, 1962. European Bronze Age Shields, *Proceedings of the Prehistoric Society* 28, 156-190.

J M Coles, P Leach, S C Minnitt, R Tabor and A S Wilson, 1999. A later Bronze Age shield from South Cadbury, Somerset, England, *Antiquity* 73, 33-48.

R Tabor, 1999. South Cadbury: Milsom's Corner, *Current Archaeology* 163, 251-255.